A B

sentimen

thought

my love

Penny

12.25.78

7-26-82

COMING CLOSE TO THE EARTH

BOOKS BY ROD McKUEN

POETRY
AND AUTUMN CAME
STANYAN STREET & OTHER SORROWS
LISTEN TO THE WARM
IN SOMEONE'S SHADOW
CAUGHT IN THE QUIET
FIELDS OF WONDER
AND TO EACH SEASON
COME TO ME IN SILENCE
MOMENT TO MOMENT
CELEBRATIONS OF THE HEART
BEYOND THE BOARDWALK
THE SEA AROUND ME . . .
COMING CLOSE TO THE EARTH

COLLECTED POEMS
TWELVE YEARS OF CHRISTMAS
A MAN ALONE
WITH LOVE . . .
THE CAROLS OF CHRISTMAS
SEASONS IN THE SUN
ALONE
THE ROD MC KUEN OMNIBUS
HAND IN HAND
THE WORKS OF ROD MC KUEN, VOL. 1

PROSE
FINDING MY FATHER

COLLECTED LYRICS
NEW BALLADS
PASTORALE
THE SONGS OF ROD MC KUEN
GRAND TOUR

coming close to the earth

ROD McKUEN

CHEVAL BOOKS
—
SIMON AND SCHUSTER
NEW YORK

Copyright © 1978 by Montcalm Productions, Inc.
Copyright © 1977 by Rod McKuen
All rights reserved
including the right of reproduction
in whole or in part in any form
Published by Simon and Schuster
A Division of Gulf & Western Corporation
Simon & Schuster Building
Rockefeller Center
1230 Avenue of the Americas
New York, New York 10020

First published in Great Britain, 1977
by Elm Tree Books Ltd.

Some of the material in this book is from
Finding My Father © 1976 by Rod McKuen.

"Goodbye" is excerpted from a book in progress © 1975,
1977 by Rod McKuen and Montcalm Productions.

International copyright secured.
First Edition

Further information may be obtained by contacting the
Cheval/Stanyan Company, 8440 Santa Monica Boulevard,
Los Angeles, CA 90069, USA, or Elm Tree Books Ltd.

Jacket photograph and design by Hy Fujita
Inside drawings and design by Hy Fujita and Rod McKuen

Manufactured in the United States of America

1   2   3   4   5   6   7   8   9   10

Library of Congress Cataloging in Publication Data
McKuen, Rod.
   Coming close to the earth.
   "Cheval books."
   I.   Title.
PS3525.A264C65   1978   811'.5'4   78-13030
ISBN 0-671-24298-9
ISBN 0-671-24627-5 (deluxe)

"So soon it passes our earthly renown."

Thomas à Kempis

The Imitation of Christ

CONTENTS

Since the initial debut three years ago of Finding My Father, *each volume of my sea trilogy has been delayed a year in the United States.*

In mid-July 1977, I completed and sent off to Great Britain the manuscript of Coming Close to the Earth. *It had been rewritten twice from my own needs and I was to revise it yet again before its October publication in England.*

In the intervening year I've agonized over the book as it first appeared. While its success meant much to me, it didn't change an ongoing feeling that I still needed to come to terms more cohesively with the story I originally set out to tell.

Finally, while working this past winter in the USSR I realized that if the book was to come out in America this year as planned, I'd have to have a go at it one more time.

What has emerged is not just a reorganized version of Coming Close to the Earth, *but the telling of a story that happened. To achieve that I've added much new material—poetry and prose. The words, old and new, are now in their correct order and, I hope, make better sense.*

For their patience I am indebted to Nan Talese, my editor in New York, who was willing to wait, and Colin Webb, her counterpart in England, who allowed me the 'state of grace' to interrupt the completion of the final volume in the trilogy, so that I might redefine the middle work. The English edition was dedicated to Brian Stone, "because he taught me fences can be broken. Even mended." This edition bears a different inscription; it is essentially a different book—now that I have learned how to tell the event as it happened.

A book is never finished, but this is as close as I will ever come to completing this one.

Rod McKuen
New York City
July 1978

CONTINUATION

My head is turning slowly
now unhurried like this April day.
I expect that in the year
                    yet upcoming
I will somewhere, if not here,
            once again sleep warm.

PROWLING

Think back. And so I do.

How did it start? How did it start to end? How could a thing so worked for and so well built fall? There were signals, signposts, maps. Why did I ignore each signal, each sign?

As painful as retelling is, I have to do it for myself. And so I start to reconstruct, rebuild, the life pulled down around me, hoping I can make the replaced structures stand just long enough to find a single answer: why?

Each of us is earthbound, coming from the stars or wading to the shore. Sailing out, we must sail back—even if the voyage stops upon the ocean's bottom or beyond the universe. If there is rest at all, we take our ease not on some distant star or in the middle ocean. The notion that the earth is merely a departing place is hardly worth the time it takes to say so. Heaven and hell may fire our imagination, but surely ground and ground alone is home.

Dialogue cannot be broken, communication lines must never be upended. If we make space within our heads then we should take care to arrive at each and every space we seek, together.

I was sure that what we had, however large or little, was enough to bring us closer to the earth. I need the warm ground for comfort and most of all reality.

WHISTLE STOPS

I go out slowly first,
             tentative,
like a bather testing water,
I scrutinize the night.
Will the dangers this time
outnumber the rewards?

Where I have been
impatient in past lives
I am content just now
to venture slowly, if at all
into the darkness.

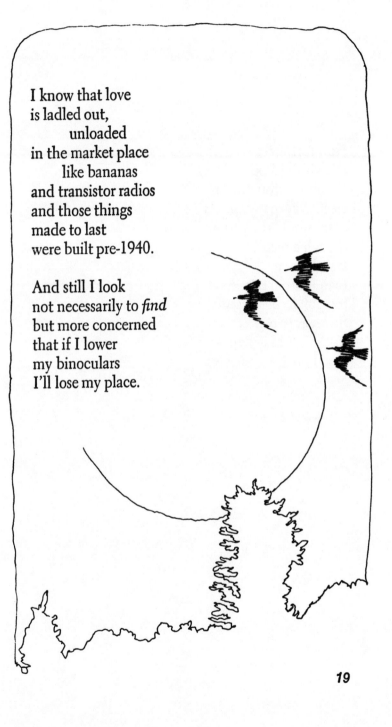

I know that love
is ladled out,
        unloaded
in the market place
        like bananas
and transistor radios
and those things
made to last
were built pre-1940.

And still I look
not necessarily to *find*
but more concerned
that if I lower
my binoculars
I'll lose my place.

How fortunate
the whistle stops
  and factory towns
elect to keep my secrets
as they hold their own,
though a secret
is little more
than information
too dull to be passed
from ear to ear
    as gossip—
 too boring to be news.

Increasingly
if it were up to me
        I'd hide nothing
except my face
in private pillows.
For I have almost no one
                to protect.
And yet I'm glad
that cities still
continue as our guard
        and guardian.

I've stayed within
           my rabbit hole
too late, too long.
Perhaps I now enjoy
the solitude
I always fought
so hard against.

What have I learned
as I've gone traveling?
That I'd lie motionless
          forever maybe
or die easily
within some known
          or unknown arms
that wrap me up
and leave me
for the morning's mischief.

One more man, I am
trying every way I know
to make it through
even one more day.

DINOSAURS

A string untied
needs tying up.
As every empty space,
to merely prove
its own existence,
needs walking through.

Dinosaurs
once walked the earth
            but where?
I haven't been there.

How many comets
        have I charted
as they arched across
the winter sky, then fell?
None has fallen
near enough for me to see
the well dug by its impact.

The ancient
and the accessible
vie for my attention.

Dinosaurs
have given way
to drive-ins
their outside hulks
no different
from each other.
Their rib cages
        then and now—
fast food devoured by
the smaller animals.

REACH DOWN

I grasp
a handful
of good ground
in doing so
I touch the heel
and the toe of God,
the arteries of angels.

Best of all
by coming closer
to the earth
I see myself
the way I should be.

EARLY IN THE EARTH

Entry Two: A Statement

You fill me with anxiety and that is better than not being filled at all. You open up your life to me—could I ask more. I have no quarrel with the men who've loved you, only appreciation for their taste.

I believe that every time we love or try to love, unconsciously we seek out duplicates, probably with help from someone else because the cloning is not always obvious. Then again there are those rare times when opposites like magnets pull us forward. Maybe this was such a time.

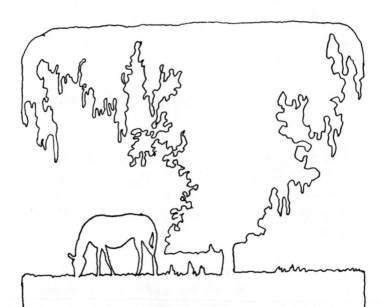

THE FIRST TIME

Beyond the trees
of what the world
terms wilderness
there is a first time.
Not to be confused
with anything
that's yet to happen
or what has gone before.

It feels not merely more,
but all there must be
                all there is.

Skating on your smile
                    each night
I know that I am safe.
And I am privileged beyond
whatever God there is
to watch with you
the man-made stars
and those the master
scatters out himself.

Far off
unpeopled planets
dart the heavens.
If I can glide
along your grin
the other worlds
were truly made
              for only us.

Away from you
I don't exist,
nothing's true
or even false.
I've no one
to dress up for
no reason
to leave home
or even share what's left to share.
It must be that the learning stops
now that I've learned to learn
                    with you.

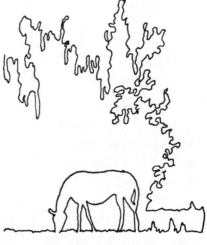

MORE WINE

Drunk I love you
sane or sober
until the wine of wanting
passes from the vintage
          to the dregs.

And as the carpenters
and the village vintner's son
make up the casks again
aiming for some year ahead,
we fill ourselves
with one another
vintage wine enough.

And now a toast;
I wish you heady harvests
every day of every year,
no unsure hours
or sleepless nights
and earth enough
when you're in cities
to make the valleys
            of New England
and all the greenest hills
                in France
stay forever green
inside your heart.

A LINE OF ANTS

A line of red-black ants
disappear below the corner
          of the house.
Their single file trail
followed backwards
leads across an open space
precarious at best.

The open space
a gravel driveway
where no bridge permit
has been requested.

I've got till six,
        no later,
to plan diversions—
a belt of honey
in a safe direction
sugar spilled across the lawn
to start the worker ants
skirmishing and stumbling
        to safety,
before you come driving home.

To keep you from the guilt
of even little murders,
my sleeves are rolled
and in my head
a battle plan
is starting.

A single line
of red-black ants
has given this long day
of separation, purpose.

NOON AGAIN

Your thighs
are like a hidden
          honeycomb
as we move
closer now.

How is it that the bee
has left your legs
          untouched
surely he can smell
the sweetness
          waiting there.

I open then your thighs
          with pride
before the sun.

You rub your belly
like Italian women
kneading bread
as I move down
between your legs
          closer still
but not as close
as I will finally be
before the noon
                takes over.

Your breathing's
full of unintended sighs.
It has no cadence now.

Has clover
ever smelled as sweet
as your warm body
growing warmer still.

Slowly now
I'll be easy
but I want to fill you up
Fuller than I've filled myself
with drink or eating.

We're floating, falling
I can't reach you.
        Yes, I can.

Breast to breast
            then down
between your thighs
another time
to outline inch by inch
that sweet triangle
always sure to bring me
            certainty in life.

Don't move.
I'll make the motions
            wide enough
to take us both
beyond the sun
and back again,
then focus on your eyes.

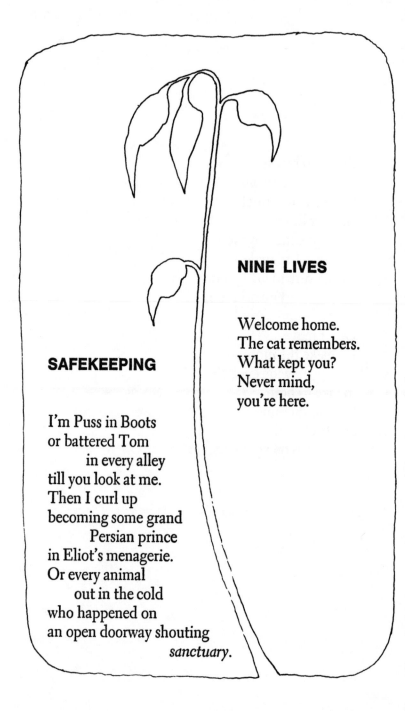

NINE LIVES

Welcome home.
The cat remembers.
What kept you?
Never mind,
you're here.

SAFEKEEPING

I'm Puss in Boots
or battered Tom
     in every alley
till you look at me.
Then I curl up
becoming some grand
     Persian prince
in Eliot's menagerie.
Or every animal
     out in the cold
who happened on
an open doorway shouting
           sanctuary.

ATLANTIC AND PACIFIC

Two cats adopted us
one black and white
the other white and black.

You never cared for cats,
                    not really,
but I am ever grateful
that you indulged
my need for pastoral
that kitchen cats provide.

You silently forgave
their traipsing
                and trespassing
in and out of windows,
playing on the stairs
and drinking all the cream
                        you'd hidden
for your morning coffee.

By that toleration
and your tales of Saki's Tobermory
you spoke great volumes
of your love for me.

By your willingness
to learn about
and then be captured
        by a cat
you proved that even
after half a lifetime
of finding your own way
you still could help invent
a brand new common ground.

Two cats
one black and white,
another white and black.
No matter what
another book or bible says,
you have mastered shadings.
You know that grays exist.

And you have taught me
the eyelids of the
                    morning
are of a different hue
than those the sunset
          settles on us.

Two cats.
The black and white one's
          called Atlantic
the white and black, Pacific.
Since both oceans separate us
I fantasize that when I'm gone
one or the other treads through
             Little Venice
and comes home to you
to lie contented through the night
         at our bed's end.

Two lives.
And whatever comes and goes
through the garden
                or the window
they could not be closer
even at a distance.

Still for those minutes
once or twice a week
when doubt brought on by need
            comes by,
leave the window open
so Atlantic and Pacific
can ebb and flow
in their natural course.

FORTY/FORTY

Your dress is riding now
up above your knees.
Your thighs
are round and growing
as we settle on the common
my eyes go on avoiding yours,
they move along your body
settling now upon the top part
                of your legs
uncovered
out of their safe envelope
like a party invitation.

My eyes
now dart from you.
They try to find
a butterfly
a fly ball or an ocean.
Anything.

The park is sunny,
                    pigeon territory.
Can't we move
back up the stairs
where comfort is the main
                              concern?
You know the sun
hangs lower by the minute
its only thought in mind
to give you one more
                        headache.
I'll run
and get an aspirin
the tallest glass
        of water.

Come with me
both of us have had
                    the sun,
our share of stale air
                    awaits within.

I'd rather live
and go on living
by pulling deep
        into my lungs
the air you breathe
than depend on wind
from open windows.

No window opens
on a better world
than what we have
within each other's arms.

WINDMILLS ONLY

There are no dragons
                anymore
        only windmills
      nothing left
to slay except the
                clock
that goes on stealing
time from us.

No one tells
the would be Don Quixotes
how easily a windmill
chomping, churning
cutting through the air
can be stopped
or made to move
more slowly.

Who comes forth to say
the graveled growl
of these metal
wooden windmills
is only made
by old machines
rusted, needing
oil and care.

The only fire
they ever spew
            or spit
is the glint of sun
on summer Sundays
as steel
slices up
 the sky.

Not here, upstate
or even on the floor
of Scotland's lake
are there dragons
                anymore.

Should one pretend
his way into your life
stand back, take aim
                and blow.
Like some determined
birthday child
who puts the candles
on his cake
to smoldering
with a single breath,
you could send a dragon
fleeing with a wink.

Your lungs
are every bit
          as big
as those
of any windmills
on the farm
or in the
barnyard
down the road.
But anyway,
there are no dragons
          anymore.

SILENT AS THE STONES

Entry Three: Changing Course

A compass is a small thing, trapped amid the panel's instruments or resting in the hand. I'm not sure any compass knows the truth—any more than all or any of us knows what's real or facsimile. The needle hasn't quivered, but I think the vessel's changing course. Where it's bound for I'm not sure, but it will go on pounding through the seas till every sea's been sailed.

Call me or send a message in a bottle. I'll be within the next port waiting. Always in the harbor.

NAMES, 1

Placing my hand upon your shoulder
and slowly with my other hand
taking yours to lead you,
right or wrong or in between,
I care not what the populace
cautions or gives warning—
kindness I'll return in kind, because you care.

Did you know that every hour
each minute given over to me
verifies the way I feel toward you
over again and over.
Songs you make by smiling,
jigs you dance by lying still,
oceans we cross just by
looking at them from both windows.
Isn't it a miracle?

NAMES, 2

Right or wrong
only God
dare make a judgment.

Maybe you're unsure
come close then
kill me quietly
unless you feel
enough is nothing or
nothing is enough.

NAMES, 3

From the top of our high bedroom
I watch both bay and ocean.
Rhymes are absent here
each initial starts a name.

If you read me
Send your arms   to tell me.
Let loose your limbs
and I will know
needs are not confined
day by day to me.

Promises to keep
islands to be found
nothing can go wrong
everything we need
surrounds us and abounds.

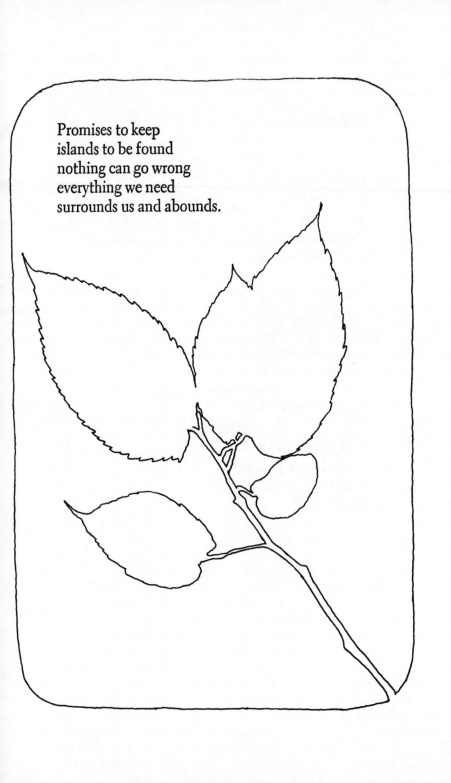

DISCOVERY

Hold on to me
as no one has
while we settle
soft and simple
amid the city grass.

I ask that you
stay long enough
to help me prove
that I have worth
    of some kind.
        You decide.
Am I narrow as the
           noontide,
am I high enough
to touch a single star?
Will I ever reach
the far field?

Do I have worth enough
to occupy an hour
            maybe more
within the frame of reference
            you call time.

Two people living
giving out the best
            to one the other
                a handshake
or a double handstand
taken to its farthest
and most perfect resting place.

The corners of your eyes
but just the corners—
            frown.
Your nipples now erect
nudge your dress
as if to burrow through.
You haven't smiled
and yet you do.

I wish that I were
          plain enough
to show you I'm but me
or as *fancy* as I feel
you think I should be.

Can you carry me
across the water,
turn and run
along the sand
with me
our feet not touching even spray
                this time.

Help me.

Sort me out
while I divine what's real
        or make believe
            in you.

Better still deliver me
if not to your own self
then to the midnight's
        other side.

I could now be saved
by hearing you say no
as surely as salvation lies
on the velvet forehead
        of a yes.

STILL RUNNING
(This time into August)

I loom over you
for one long moment,
before I fall
to play
       and plunge
           and pillage.

I must have been
            a pirate
in some other life.

If the heart
was truly at its prayer
I think I heard it
       speak a word
make a sign so softly
it might have been amen.
Or was the word again.

You may well be
the one to show me
the survival route
by teaching me the way
       away from you.

CONTRAST

I know love
by its first name
and living by its last.

I'm not afraid
of what's upcoming
or what has gone before
and if there's nothing
left to know about or learn
I'll review the early lessons
                yet again:

But please
don't turn the light switch yet
as valuable and friendly
as the darkness is
leave the porch light on
                for contrast.

PRISONER BEYOND THE TREES

I meant, I mean
to take you to the trees
or the tree country—
as I have planned consistently
to push you beachward.

The trees,
the seashores wait
while I lie next to you
in bed and wonder
will the trees
be tall enough
to make you happy?
The beaches
wide enough and sandy?
The cliffs along the coastline
as beautiful as those
you're used to
on your home-ground
          outings?

Beyond the obvious
I have no reasons
as to why you've seen
                    so little
of the California coast
each time you travel here.
I am not ashamed
to show you off
to anyone and all—
                    I glory
seeing your reflection
coming back to me
from other people's eyes.

SUN SONG

The sun is in full flight
                but hovering,
guarding us
and saying *I approve*.

Your bare shoulders
brown like brown.
And now you move,
turn slowly
so that I might see
the bottoms of your feet
then move my eyes
the length and breadth
of your whole body.

The sun's approval
won so easily
and he's been making
love to you all day.

Aware of my turn now
he slips behind a cloud.

Riding home
from St. Giles Church
I made a new
cantata for you.
All brass and heavy
but gentle with Cuban rhythm,
something you might
bend and sway to
underneath tomorrow
or the next day's sun.

MY FRIEND AND FIVE STAR FINAL

Frogs croak out
each new edition
as dragonflies supply
the news past noon.

It is left
not only to the morning glory
but field mice in that old
                                  fraternity
of sly reporters
filching hill and field alike
to finally flush out
                        all the news.

Better than the radio
                    they are
the morning paper
or the grocery handout.

Sometimes I feel
that you invented media
enlisting frogs and dragonflies
as cub reporters and carriers.

The news
comes home to me,
good or bad.
Best of all
from one
who cares enough
to let me know
of tragedies
and triumphs
equal and
with love
so I never
have to fear
the Tribune
or The Times
from someone
       else.

In the summer months
Your well-paid staff
whispers hard
and tells me all.

Look!
here comes
a dragonfly reporter
          now.

Too late.
There he goes
on wings of wonder.
Never mind
You'll see him later
in the re-write room.

LITTLE EARTHQUAKES

Entry Four: Times

To write about you isn't easy. Compare it to a blind that on its spring flaps up to smash the window casing. To praise or talk about you would do more injury than compliment.

Within my own heart's head, I remember sun in California, mid-Manhattan corridors and hotel beds, a Sunday walk within Miami's mall. Island nights of fireflies and lightning.

Some pages in my diary are blotted or unused. Those must have been the happiest of times, for who can jot down happiness when it is happening? Bad times? Sure.

Still in this year together I have never once considered life or lifetime to be anything but synonymous with you.

ISLANDER

Though I've been
            an islander
most all my life,
I could sail
around the world
            on *yes*,
if you'd once use it.

How long should I wait?
How long can I wait?
As long as it takes
for you to master
north and south
and all the other
mathematical gadgetry
contained within a compass.

FENCES

They try
to build high walls,
fences, hedges even
to lock us from each other.
I can't say why
they're so concerned
or even threatened
by the needs we have,
not known to them.

Have you noticed
that our good companions
seem bent on being masons,
trying hard to make
their own foundations—
even newer dwelling places
                    for us?

A waste of time
to tell them
that our boundaries
        are the world.
We've built buildings
brick by brick together.

I am sorry to report
to those who'd lock us up or out
that we will not ignore each other,
our jailers and our keepers, yes—
but not each other.

Let the constables
know for certain
that even if they be
our kin or brothers
the only true authority,
pistol belt and badge
we acknowledge and approve
is the one or ones
of our design.

Should we be fenced
from one another for a time
we'll live *alone* on short grass
till we're able to deliver
                    bales and bounties
ladles and large boxes
              of replenished love
through the bars
and up each other's
              fire escapes
and second-story windows.

THOUGHT

I love you enough
to let you run

but
far too much
to let you
fly.

COMING CLOSE

I meant so
to bend the bough
but never once
to break the branch.

I hoped
that I might see
the blossoms
      fall intact
without the petals
              coming loose
or even once detached.

What I wanted most
          was love
in a straight
straightforward way.

I wanted you
not as you could be
had I made you up
but the way I found you
no different from
the way you really are.

I thought by now
we might have earned
a chance to come down close
and lie against the earth.

But I'm convinced
the earth will not allow
even its truest lovers
membership straight away.

I cannot care
a little for you.
I love you only just enough
to love you all the way.

HE

I've memorized my face so well
I need no mirror when I shave
And so I know that I cannot compete
with what your ever watchful eye
tells me that you need.

If I am not
to be the one
I'll settle for no less
than some assurance
that the plowboy, cowboy
            or the soldier
the helper or the helping hand
            the final man,
is the one that you deserve
to serve you and for you to serve
throughout the days remaining
            in your life.

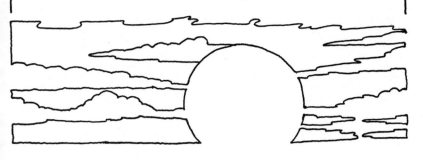

CONCRETE

Entry Five: Target Practice Revisited

I am not sure if I hit the target or the target turned, took careful aim and fired at me.

We connected in the New York winter, over again and over again proving that the aim was sure and true, or perhaps that adversaries can be controlled, corralled at will. The enemy can be confused, a smile in his direction or a well-turned frown can win not just a battle, but the war.

But I would rather speak of love than dwell on any enemy. I loved and still I love—often it's like rolling down a hill. Speed, as sure as any drug, propels me forward.

Shots are fired and if the winding down of love can kill, I'm dying even now.

TAKING AIM

Spring began its early reach
                 and all of us
went groggy, sleepless
to the docks on Sunday.

Even as we walked
              helloing everybody
the wind of winter
still held on
not fooled by sunshine.

Three days later
we'd be darting
        doorway to doorway
caught by unexpected
                 mid-week rain.
Winter hadn't left
nor had the spring begun
just because of one long
        sunshine Sunday.

Then,
I don't think it was any time
                        before that day,
I realized that I was being
carried on a cloud
sometimes gray or black
never white like snow.

I was the target
and the aim was true
no one missed me once.

It took so many months
for a single bruise
        to show itself
I might have died
without an outward blemish.
Now the rupture
on the inside
is every bit as true
and tangible
            as spitting blood.

Never step into the ring
when the flag is up,
                or the flag is waving.
Only when the flag is down.

I wish the rules for everything
were printed in the daily paper,
spelled out on billboards
                ten feet high
or taught to us in school.
Reading, writing, arithmetic
                        and *rules*
not needed just to pass
the contest or the course
but to get us through
our time allotted here.

The rules and reasons
keep on changing.

I thought at times
my enemies were strangers,
in revolving doors
of my own making
then not strangers anymore.

I suppose they call it
                target practice
because nobody wants
or needs perfection.
I do.
In the small things.
The sureness of appointments
                and the promise kept.
The knowledge that
I'm in control
not always of the circumstance
but surely of the stance,
so that I can traverse clouds
yet one more time.

No doubt I'll be back.
The firing squad
will find me waiting
unarmed except for one small book
                        of rules.

CHANGES

Even if I could conquer
muzzle or throw off
     jealousy and pride
I doubt we might have found
a meeting place.
How can something
come from nothing?
(What happened
to the everything
I was sure you'd given
         me?)

There is the envy,
       to be like you.
To take a soper or a half
and just hang easy
while you compound lies
and know I know it.
That would have been the optimum,
the top and bottom
the in most in between.

Caught in my love for you
        I dangle here
not so much in space
as the lack of it.

Once caught,
I should have said,
no love lives here
not even pity
or bewilderment.
But something hurts.

I run home to sleep
while you seek out
your Biblical David.
Your staff and crutch,
costing you nothing,
because I doubt
that you have ever
paid for pain.

SEVENTY-SEVENTH STREET, 1977

Women in doorways
breasts heaving heavy
slow—sometimes not at all.
The first long day of spring
has beat, confused them all.

Twittering fans
made from the morning paper
say whatever must be said.
The women make no words.

Men staring out,
hanging out,
of second-story windows
scratch themselves,
pat their stomachs.

Will the weather break?
Everyone says *no*,
even subway trains
coming from the ground,
              now overhead,
                 agree.

Babies go on
crying in their cradles,
kids on play streets
hijack city hydrants
and soak themselves.
Adults look on in envy.

*Ready or not
here I come.*

A hundred thousand
grandmas rock away
on as many porches.

Now the men
are back again
at window sills
beer cans in each hand.
When autumn comes
                 for sure
I'll join a gym.

Today I'd like to know
the face of someone, anyone
I could blame my headache on.

MONDAY LETTER

Your letter read
two times, no three
surprised me only
that you took the time
           to write it.

Perhaps it was a form
that you'd composed before,
something to be set down quickly
as you raced toward
tomorrow and the landing.
A marine log maybe.

I found it
half past noon
not soon enough
to question you
but late enough
to keep from calling
down the boardwalk
hello out there
I'm pitiful and sorry.

Pitiful that I need
friendship bad enough
to look for it
from those who live their lives
at such a speed
they seldom make
an understanding pause.

Sorry
because my mistakes
are many and uneven.
Even so, *hello out there*
                    I wish
you knew me better
I wish *I* knew me better.

I wish most of all
for both of us
you hadn't stopped
within your flight
to write a one-page
form-like letter.

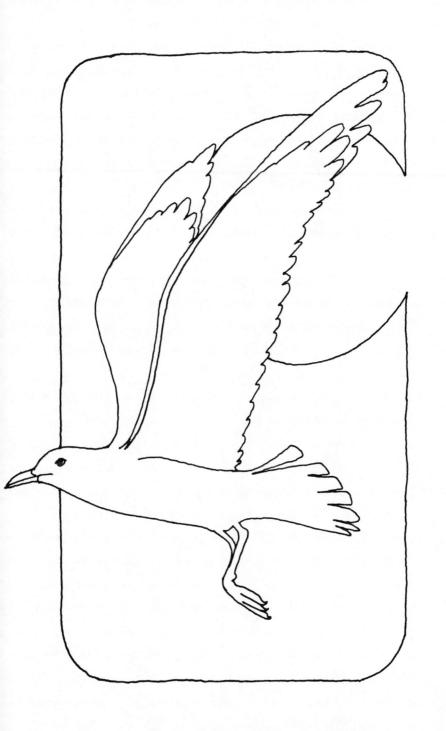

HOTEL ANSONIA POEMS

From Another Notebook

I've started keeping notes again so that I'll remember how it's happening and happened.

March, Friday

I lugged a brand new phonograph—purchased just that day—some records bought at every port of entry we stopped at as we traveled down the bright Dalmatian coast. There were tapes, unheard by anyone but me, made up especially for the guest of honor at your party. The taxi driver wouldn't help unload the boxes from the cab. As I came into the lobby, the desk clerk didn't seem to know if you lived there. The boxes were cumbersome and heavy. A kind man stopped, asking, no insisting, he could help. He did. Up the elevator we came, loaded with the boxes, to your door.

It was then that I felt foolish trying to bring your party quiet music. I had erred.

Your friends, I knew but one or two, were careful with me. Mostly they ignored me—in self-defense, I think.

Tired, I was, and sleepy. You said, "We'll just stay here."

Later, could half an hour have passed? I watched you looking, then disappearing in the kitchen with someone I hadn't seen before.

I did not cry out, though I could have. I continued to be company, one of the assorted, invited guests. I sat down for a time, not missed, but wondering how to make a decent exit dragging all those boxes out the door again.

While I was waiting, I was hoping you might pass by and in your quiet voice again say, Stay. It didn't happen and the loading up began. Before I left I wrote some words in a book I'd sent you months ago—one you hadn't opened. It sat there virgin with a dozen others, all made with special dedications.

How can there be an ending when nothing of importance has begun?

I wrote that in the book, went out the door, down the hall into the elevator through the lobby to a corner taxi and disappeared past Lincoln Center. Too numb to even think that I was going home, alone yet one more time. In that time I wanted to believe that it was over finally. Done.

MOVIES

You look out at me
from screens now wider
than the widest discard bed,
folding over and over
into strange men's arms
bounding down,
          then up again.
Is there no part of them
that you're afraid to touch?

I know that strangers
sitting solitary
in shade-pulled rooms,
pants unzipped
or standing, lying
rolling in a ball
          of darkness
feel for those
twelve-odd minutes
that you're their private
pleasure, treasure chest.

I am able now
to watch detached
outside myself
not wishing it were me
being taken up into
the warm insides of you
where I've lived
so many times before.

I admit
the first time wasn't easy
seeing you in living color
living out on celluloid
imagination or reality.

But finally
your body reaching out to me
from that so silent screen
became not real
but more a flower
narcissus-like,
some kind of curiosity
drawing me inside
your magic circle.

Once I hoped that we
might walk together
down all the well-lit streets
so that rumors would begin
to clang around us
ensuring no mistake
on the part of those
who live on fantasies
                their own
or those that you
or even I
provide for them:
that you belong to me
and we belong, are strong,
                together—
even if I sometimes feel
it isn't so, I know it is.

THE TRAVELING MAGIC SHOW

1.
Thank you
for the magic show
perfect to the last detail.
Flowers, fish and tambourines
side-show scenes
I might have missed,
had I been
the country bumpkin
leaning up against
          your door.

Things I would have only guessed at
if we hadn't hit head on
smoking up the subtlety
that most prefer to work out
               for themselves.

Nothing to chance
now there's a magician
someone who'll jump
in your brother's pants
while teaching him
                    long division.

After all the tricks
and turns are done,
the saddest thing
about a magic show,
is that the gypsy wagon travels
down the road,
                    is gone.

Even those who sneak
beneath the tent for free
feel cheated.
One more illusion please
another scarf
        from out the sleeve.

Simple men sometimes conceal
genius in their ears and pockets
a rabbit in the hat,
scarves with dazzling colors
appear and disappear
                    from nowhere
bright balloons from Brigadoon
pigeons, doves and other birds
come from eyes and ears
                    and noses.
In other words, not only birds
but who in life turns out to be
what anyone supposes?

2.
Is there some kind of in between?
A way for us to reach beyond
the buildings and the bullshit
                    to reality?
Reality for you
is something different
          than it is for me.

Surely there's a meeting place,
a common ground, an in between.
Sailing seaward's not the answer,
as yet we have but little knowledge
                    of the sky.
Perhaps the closer we can stay to earth
the better chance we'll have of being
what each of us as individuals
                    need in someone else.

I think that's true.
I wish it to be so.
Or I wish something old
or still within the realm of new
that would keep the pleasure
you bring home to me safe
while driving off the pain.

Pleasure is the best
of all things possible—
but for those few moments
                    stolen or a gift
the payback is so difficult
that I doubt any of us
would go forward into joy
if we knew the price.

DAVID

You were an enigma.
I used to feel sorry
for the trouble
I might have caused you.
Now I know you thrived,
                    survived
lived, made love on troubles
I was having.
You and your accomplice,
a velvet suited pair
I think you taught each other
magic and monstrosities
not solicited or asked for.
How to lie in small ways
how to steal the larger things
like feelings, hope
and that most personal
                    of properties
the love that others share.

I understand that real love
is not within your ken
but jesus how you do excel
in thoughtlessness,
self pity and destruction.
I even think
you only run to one another
        out of desperation
when no one else will have you.
That must be often now.

I see you both
throughout eternity
side by side not sighing
or even in the act of love
but telling lies to one another.

Beautiful people
staying pretty on the outside
to attract new prey.
But inside hiding somewhere
is a sketch, a small relief
if not the detailed portrait
of a masculine/feminine Dorian Gray.

BADLANDS

What you're buying,
                trolling for,
in The Badlands
every summer Sunday
I could give you
if you'd let me try.
Even mystery, I swear.
You've but to learn
that mystery and magic
are only sleight of hand.

Stand still long enough
to let me prove to you
an update on your life's
                in order.
There ought to be
        a plan.

I should leave you
        to yourself
but how can I look on
as you allow your life
to flow along the gutter
and disappear toward
        the nearest drain.

How can I have loved
        or love you
and not care
that what I love

not only slips from me
but daily flies
        from its own self?

Alike we are
in many things.
Too proud to beg forgiveness
        close at hand—yet dying
when the door is closed.

There seems to be
so much of you to share,
so many pieces of the pie
are cut and squared
before the plate
is passed to me.

I never felt
that I should stamp
S.P.Q.R. across your back
or any pride of ownership.

Love doesn't thrive
on harnesses however hitched.

I only felt
that I should have
        the lion's share
because I knew
I loved you more;
as now I know
that being loved
is not enough for you
you need the adulation
of the crowd
on Broadway
        or the badlands.

I should have been
    the faithful cowboy,
you the horse.
At suppertime
the horse comes home.

Perhaps in times
                  yet coming
it will be enough for me
to know that you were mine
even in the dead of night
when you were here on loan.
A sorcerer's apprentice
you always made me feel
you were here
without condition.

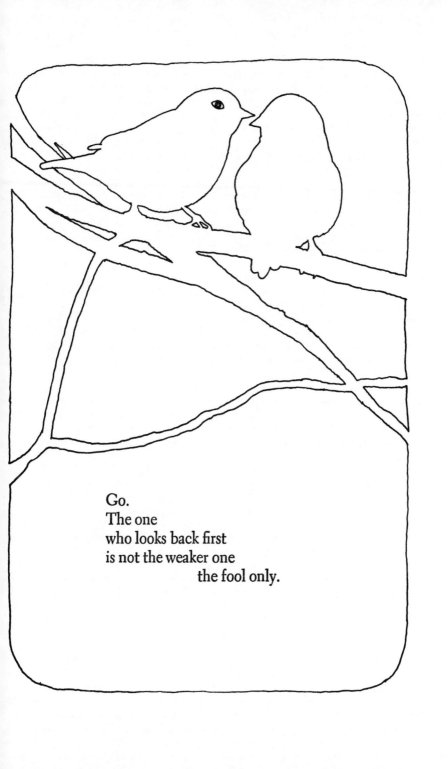

Go.
The one
who looks back first
is not the weaker one
            the fool only.

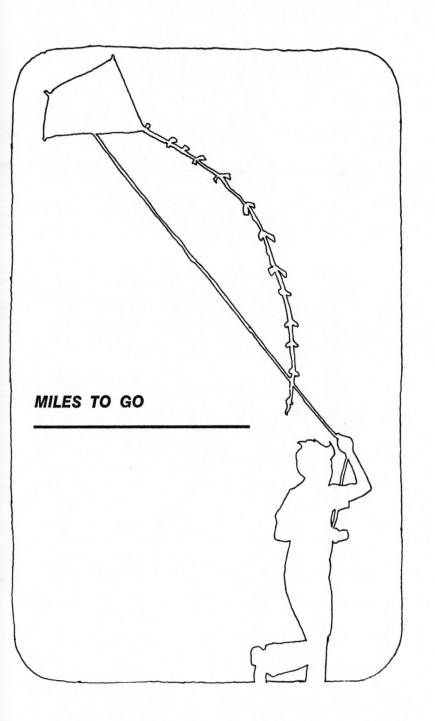

MILES TO GO

Entry Six: Goodbye

Once you said we have nothing to laugh at together. Meanwhile you laugh at me enough for both of us. You clean me out of kindness, slowly, till there's little left. The difference in us is that should I have to change for you, I'm willing. But I want you only as you are. If I don't agree with you, or question you at all, I need help. If I do agree, then I have no opinion of my own.

I said we'd never say goodbye. Today the word comes easy and without effort. Maybe that's because I don't have to say it face to face to you. We're at either ends of telephone lines again. A bad connection.

I love you still. As much, and as love goes, even more than that first half-drunk night you concentrated so hard on pleasing me and did.

I love you. I am not afraid to say it, even after all the mean and misery that's passed between us.

Apologies are not enough I know. How could they compensate for rides across the ocean and the continent done in tears and not in laughter? How could they make up for Saturday soldiers battling one the other, wounding words spit out machine-gun like, or two people desperately in need of one the other not making up? But I apologize for leading you, not letting you love me in your way—at arm's length. For rushing you, not stopping once to read your needs, thinking I'd fulfilled them each time you filled mine. For intimidation—if that's what it was—or being timid and unsure, pretending I was strong when my strength only came from you. For making you think every night in bed was one more potential crisis. It never was. It never was anything but the very best. Even when I knew you forced yourself to bring yourself to me. I never felt anything but happiness and honor, joy and a letting go. No one else has yet come close to giving me that feeling.

Goodbye. I love you and I'll go on loving. I will change as you will change. I wish you Christmas every time your eyes close. I pray that you will run with deer and soar with eagles, touching on the ground only long enough to find that man who'll love you every bit as much as I do and one you'll feel the same toward.

It is still early in the day for each of us. Despite the darkness up ahead, I know there will be someone to lead you through the dark and someone you can lead. That it wasn't me is something less important than your finding that one to your liking. I only hope while you were adding to my life, I haven't interrupted anything within yours.

AHEAD

Who brings home
                    the torch
the winner or the loser?
Is the beginning
where the race starts
and the ending
just another way of saying
Stop the clock
and let's begin again?

The only time
I come out the winner
is when I race myself
and pass the mark
I've set before.

The trophies I collect
                    are smiles.

The only ribbons
I could safely stretch
across my chest
would be those
to bind my heart
and keep it from pounding
            into nothingness
when I felt loved.

144

I don't compete.
I'm lesser than no man
and I've found no one better.
I know all creatures,
                beings, people
to be unalike.

How can I compete,
win or lose a race
with someone other
                than myself.
Being me is hard enough
but someone other, never.

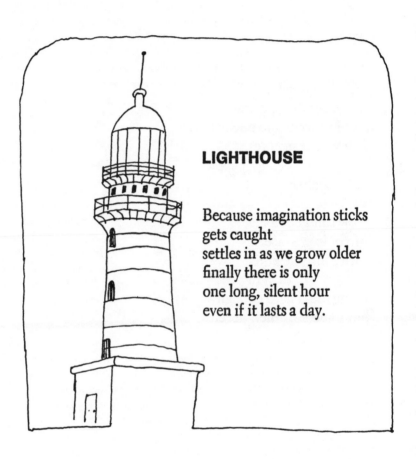

LIGHTHOUSE

Because imagination sticks
gets caught
settles in as we grow older
finally there is only
one long, silent hour
even if it lasts a day.

Have we been living
all our years for this?
It may be so.
It well may be
the size of life
is measured by the hours,
years and days it takes
for each of us to turn
within the circle
of the slowest dance.

Where then and why
how does the eagle
or the falcon fly?
And if the rabbit runs
does he run forward
                or run back?

The eagle
and the falcon too
are foragers,
          but self-propelled.

Lucky rabbit
always running to its lair
and always, always
          finding something there.

I think perhaps
that we are running, yes.
Always away and not toward.

I think that we are looking
not quite for the end
but for a slow dance done
upon the killing ground.

The damage we inflict
in love or hate
or any other name it's given
is usually beyond repair.

What then can we give
or promise one the other?
Ourselves? We try,
but always we hold back.
More promises?
So few are kept
that credibility
must now be stitched
or sewn together.

Finally, the answer
comes up once again,
we can offer one another
nothing but the rattle
of destructive words
a slow death
on the killing ground.
So much for love
        and mornings.

THE STORM

The storm has widened
till now it stretches out
across the sky from end to end.
The thunder isn't thunder anymore
it must be God
in some caprice or slight displeasure
licking at the ends of clouds.

The rain, once quiet
    in the early evening
makes waterfalls outside each window.

The wind? God again,
this time breathing hard
letting go great gusts of air
that swallows leaves
      from every tree
and carries them
in close armada
down the gutter rivers
to clog each drain
      and drainpipe.

In winter
this would be a blizzard
and if in absentmindedness
      or impatience
he stubs his toe
or stomps his foot
God almighty will have made
      on this May night
an earthquake that will go on
rumbling down the ages.

Curiously the streets
are not uncrowded.
Umbrella people stride upright
those caught unaware
hunch over and go nowhere
        or go home.

Do they know
this is no ordinary storm
but such a curiosity
that man who can't explain
                the elements
siphon into scriptures
and call miracles?

I brave the rain.
No. The streams of water
falling on my face
and my brave shoulders
as I stand naked
    in the backyard
searching out the secrets
of the still beclouded sky.

I have counted moons
magnified them
in a Moscow glass,
charted constellations
                in the tropics
and shared great armfuls
of dim and distant stars
in my own flatlands
with no one but myself.

A storm is not to stop me.

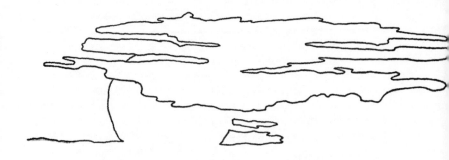

Though my skyward vision
            blurs just now
I feel that I can pierce the sky
see through anything
to its certain center.
 (A vanity to be sure,
and one of many,)
but I have looked
      so hard and long
I'm now astronomer by assimilation
astrologer of sorts by my own will.

It's fitting somehow
that only God—
not even me, myself—
knows what I'm looking for.

Something's surely missing
in the life that I attempt
to live
until I find it
it can have no name.

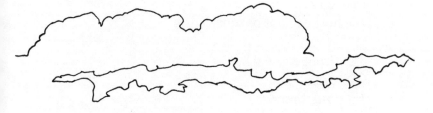

And now it's clearing,
a flash of light
and one last
heavenly thunder laugh.

The ground has had
a good long drink.
I stay within the night air
still.
Something's out here. Somewhere.

ASSESSMENT

In coming back again
in mind and matter
have I learned anything?
        I think not.
The ache is still
as deep as ever,
the hurt will not be muzzled.

I'm stronger though.
Time does that,
time and thunder.
I pray to God
I'll go on looking
always with a sense of hope
          and wonder.

ASPIRATION

Never satisfied
we turn from earth
            to heaven.
Knowing we're not
                angels yet
we pray aloud,
not proud but sure
that given one more hour
another day perhaps
a time of concentration
we'll rise up
surpass, surprise ourselves
and all of our ambitions

maybe even thrust
an unclenched fist
through an empty cloud
or pass a golden galaxy
and with some patience
and no little practice
even touch the lower sky.

ROD McKUEN's *books of poetry have sold in excess of 16,000,000 copies in hardcover, making him the bestselling and most widely read poet of our times. In addition, he is the bestselling living author writing in any hardcover medium today. His poetry is taught and studied in schools, colleges, universities, and seminaries throughout the world.*

Mr. McKuen is the composer of nearly 2,000 songs, which have been translated into Spanish, French, Dutch, German, Russian, Japanese, Czech, Chinese, Norwegian, Afrikaans, and Italian, among other languages. They account for the sale of more than 180,000,000 records. His songs include "Jean," "Love's Been Good to Me," "The Importance of the Rose," "Rock Gently," "Ally Ally, Oxen Free," and several dozen songs with French composer Jacques Brel, including "If You Go Away," "Come Jef," "Port of Amsterdam," and "Seasons in the Sun." Both writers term their writing habits together as three distinct methods: collaboration, adaptation, and translation.

*His film music has twice been nominated for Motion Picture Academy Awards (*The Prime of Miss Jean Brodie *and* A Boy Named Charlie

Brown), *and his classical work, including symphonies, concertos, piano sonatas, and his very popular Adagio for Harp and Strings, is performed by leading orchestras. In May 1972, the London Royal Philharmonic premiered his Concerto No. 3 for Piano & Orchestra and a suite,* The Plains of My Country. *In 1973 the Louisville Orchestra commissioned Mr. McKuen to compose a suite for orchestra and narrator, entitled* The City. *It was premiered in Louisville and Danville, Kentucky, in October 1973 and was subsequently nominated for a Pulitzer Prize in music. He has been commissioned by the city of Portsmouth, England, for a symphonic work to commemorate the sailing of the first ships from that city to Australia. The new work will be jointly premiered in Portsmouth and Australia's Sydney Opera House. (Mr. McKuen was the first American artist to perform a series of concerts during the opera house's opening season.)*

His Symphony No. 3, commissioned by the Menninger Foundation in honor of their fiftieth anniversary, was premiered in 1975 in Topeka, Kansas, and he has appeared to sell-out houses with more than thirty American symphony orchestras.

The author has completed the libretto and music for a full-length opera, The Black Eagle.

In July 1976 two new McKuen works were premiered at St. Giles Church, Cripplegate, in the City of London. A Concerto for Cello and Orchestra and the first major symphonic composition written for synthesizer and symphony orchestra (Concerto for Balloon and Orchestra). As a balloonist he has flown in the skies above the Western United States and recently South Africa. He likes outdoor sports and driving.

Much of the author's time is now spent working for and with his nonprofit foundation Animal Concern and attempting to change laws in states and countries that allow public and private agencies to collect, but withhold, information from private citizens. Recently he has been active in attempting to ensure the passage of the Equal Rights Amendment and actively works to bring about human rights for all people. He is a founding member of the First Amendment Society.

Finding My Father was Rod McKuen's first book of prose, and he is currently at work on the third volume of his "Sea Trilogy" (Coming Close to the Earth being the second).

In 1978 Rod McKuen was named by the University of Detroit for his humanitarian work and in Washington was presented the Carl Sandburg award by the National Platform Association as "the outstanding people's poet, because he has made poetry a part of so many people's lives in this country."

For nearly a year McKuen has taken a sabbatical from concerts and touring to work on the television documentary series The Unknown War, as poet, composer of the film's score, and co-adapter, with producer Fred Wiener, of the scripts.

One of his newest projects is his first ballet, commissioned by Petrov for the Pittsburgh Ballet. It will have its premier there in May of 1979.

Having recently taken up residence in New York, the composer-poet now divides his time between Manhattan and the California coast.